THE

UNITED STATES

GOVERNED

BY

SIX HUNDRED

THOUSAND

DESPOTS

.

THE

UNITED STATES GOVERNED

BY

SIX HUNDRED THOUSAND DESPOTS

A TRUE STORY OF SLAVERY

John Swanson Jacobs

The University of Chicago Press   CHICAGO AND LONDON

The University of Chicago Press, Chicago 60637
The University of Chicago Press, Ltd., London
Published 2024
Printed in the United States of America

33 32 31 30 29 28 27 26 25 24   1 2 3 4 5

ISBN-13: 978-0-226-83300-2 (paper)
ISBN-13: 978-0-226-83301-9 (e-book)
DOI: https://doi.org/10.7208/chicago/9780226833019.001.0001

Library of Congress Cataloging-in-Publication Data

Names: Jacobs, John S., 1815–1875, author.
Title: The United States governed by six hundred thousand despots : a true
    story of slavery / John Swanson Jacobs.
Other titles: United States governed by 600,000 despots
Description: Chicago : The University of Chicago Press, 2024.
Identifiers: LCCN 2023039952 | ISBN 9780226833002 (paperback) |
    ISBN 9780226833019 (ebook)
Subjects: LCSH: Jacobs, John S., 1815–1875. | Jacobs, Harriet A. (Harriet
    Ann), 1813–1897. | African Americans—North Carolina—Biography.
    | Fugitive slaves—North Carolina—Biography. | Enslaved persons—
    North Carolina—Biography. | Enslaved persons—United States—
    Biography. | Slavery—North Carolina. | Slavery—United States.
Classification: LCC E450 .J325 2024 | DDC 973/.049607300922 [B]—dc23/
    eng/20230919
LC record available at https://lccn.loc.gov/2023039952

♾ This paper meets the requirements of ANSI/NISO Z39.48-1992
(Permanence of Paper).

Contents

THE

UNITED STATES GOVERNED

BY

SIX HUNDRED THOUSAND DESPOTS

A TRUE STORY OF SLAVERY, SHOWING:—

1. *That Brutality is inseparable from Slavery.*
2. *That the Constitution of the United States of America is the Bulwark of American Slavery.*
3. *That the only hope of abolition of Slavery is in separation from the Union.*

by a Fugitive Slave.

[About a month ago, a respectably dressed man came into the Editor's room in *The Empire* Office, and, after a modestly expressed apology, begged to be informed where he could obtain the loan of Hildreth's *History of the United States*, and a correct copy of the American Constitution, stating that he had endeavoured to purchase them at the booksellers, but had not succeeded in his enquiries. The novelty of the application at once awakened some curiosity; and the person before us had sufficient in his manner and appearance to deepen that feeling into one of abiding interest. He was a "man of colour," whose complexion would be hardly noticeable among the average specimens of the English face, about thirty-five or forty years of age, with bright intelligent eyes, a gentle firm voice, and a style of speech decidedly American. In answer to some interrogatories which the occasion suggested, he said briefly, that he was engaged in writing out his experiences of American slavery, and wanted the books in question for reference, and was prepared to deposit a sum of money in excess of their value with any one who would lend them to him. Hildreth's *History*, and the last edition of the United States' Constitution authorised by Congress, happened to be among our own office books, and they were supplied to our new acquaintance, he, on his own proposition, depositing in the hands of our office porter a bank note for £10 as security for their due return. A fortnight afterwards, the Fugitive Slave—for such he had acknowledged himself to be—again presented himself at our office to return the books; and at the same time he produced, and left in our hands the following written narrative. In publishing this "unvarnished tale," and, in many respects, really eloquent account of slavery, we have scarcely altered a word used by the writer, or done more than correct the orthography and divide it into readable sentences. The writer is in Sydney; we understand he has been among the successful gold-diggers, and is now about changing his occupation by going to sea. We shall be much mistaken, if his narrative is not read with a lively interest.—ED. *E.*]

I WAS BORN IN EDENTON, NORTH CAROLINA, one of the oldest States in the Union, and had five different owners in 18 years. My first owner was Miss Penelope Hanablue, the invalid daughter of an innkeeper. After her death I became the property of her mother. My only sister was given to a niece of hers and daughter of Dr. James A. Norcom.

My father and mother were slaves. I have a very slight recollection of my mother who died when I was quite young, though my father made impressions on my mind in childhood

that can never be forgotten. I should do my dear old grandmother injustice did I not mention her too; for there was too
great a difference between her meekness and my father's fury,
though slavery had caused it.

To be a man and not to be—a father without authority—
a husband and no protector—is far pleasanter to dream of
than to experience.

Such is the condition of every slave throughout the United
States; he owns nothing—he can claim nothing. His wife is
not his—his children are not his; they can be taken from him,
and sold at any minute, as far as the fleshmonger may see fit
to carry them. Slaves are recognised as property by the law
and can own nothing except at the consent of their masters.
A slave's wife or daughter may be insulted before his eyes with
impunity; he himself may be called on to torture them, and
dare not refuse. To raise his hand in their defence, is death by
the law. He must bear all things and resist nothing. If he leaves
his master's premises at any time without a written permit,
he is liable to be flogged; yet they say we are happy and con-
tented. I will admit that slaves are sometimes cheerful; they
sing and dance, as it is natural for any one to do when placed
in their position. I myself had changed owners four times
before I could see the policy of this. My father taught me to
hate slavery; but forgot to teach me how to conceal my hatred.

The deepest impression ever made on my mind was by
my father when I was about 7 years old. Mrs. Hanablue and
himself one day called me at the same time.

I answered her call first, then my father's. What his feelings could have been I know not, but his words were these—"John, whenever I call you again, come to me, I care not who else may call."

"Sir, my mistress had called me."

"If she is your mistress, I am your father."

He said no more—it was enough—I knew the remainder—"Honour thy father and thy mother as the Lord thy God hath commanded thee, that thy days may be prolonged, and that it may go well with thee in the land which the Lord thy God giveth thee."

What has Slavery to say to this? Does she allow children to obey their parents? No: nor the God that created them, when it does not serve their ends. The doctrine they preach to slaves is blasphemy—telling them obedience to their earthly masters is obedience to God, and that they must be obedient servants here on earth if they ever hope to enjoy eternal life hereafter.

When a little boy, my father used to take me with him to the Methodist church. I continued to go, when I could, until one Mr. Moumon came there to preach; he preached to the whites in the morning, and to the slaves in the afternoon. His discourse to the slaves was invariably about robbing henhouses and keeping everything about your master's house in good order. This is what they call religious instruction given to slaves. Not a Sunday school nor a Bible class throughout the south where a slave dare put his head in to learn anything for himself. It is unlawful for any one to teach him the alphabet, to give, sell, or lend him a Bible; yet they profess to be Christians they have churches, Bible and Tract Societies. They steal infants from their mothers to buy Bibles to send to heathens, and flog women to unpaid toil, to support their churches. This is what they do for the glory of God and the good of souls.

In 1850, I was in one of the railway coaches going from Boston Mass to Rochester N.Y. There were several ministers in the coach that had been to Boston to attend the missionary meeting, where the slave question had been discussed. Two of their number were either cut off or cut themselves loose, to save them the trouble, for having said that slavery was anti-Christian. This was bringing things too near home. They were dealing in human flesh and as a matter of course must make it appear all right in the eyes of the world. Well the Bible is taken for it. They first prove that slavery existed in the days of Christ and the Apostles; secondly, their course was non-interference, and that it was their firm belief, that a man could be a slaveholder and yet a worthy member in a Christian Church. Knowing that these gentlemen professed to be of the latter opinion, I begged leave to ask a question, after having quoted these words, "Inasmuch as ye have done it unto one of the least of these my brethren, ye have done it unto me."

"Now, sir, will you tell me which of the two are the greatest sinners in the sight of God, those who bow down and worship the image of God carved out in wood or stone, or those who sell Christ in the shambles in a human being?"

Said he, "It depends altogether upon the light they have had on the subject."

"Well, if the south has not had sufficient light on this subject, why send your missionaries from home while the people at home are in greater darkness than those to whom you send them?"

I could get no further answer from him. The fact is, there is more knaving than ignorance among them. A man that will sell his own offspring, which thousands of them have done, has shown himself unnatural enough to do anything. They admit that a negro has a soul, but it must be a very painful acknowledgment to a nation whose prejudices are so strong. Go into the free States, or rather the so-called free States, for there is not a spot in that country, from one end to the other, whence I could not be dragged into slavery. I begin at the schoolhouse, I suppose myself a father living in one of these so-called free States. We have town schools in the different wards, I am always ready to pay my tax to help support these schools, but when I send my children they are told, "We don't keep school here for niggers."

There is my poll-tax I have paid. Am I not allowed to vote? "No, we don't allow niggers at the ballot box here."

Having grown sick of such treatment, I take my wife and children and go in search of a State where they will treat us according to our behaviour and not our colour. I have paid my passage on the steamer. As soon as I step foot into the saloon, with my wife and children, I am told that "niggers are not allowed here."

"But, sir, I have a cabin-ticket."

"I don't care for that, I tell you niggers are not allowed here."

The boat lands. I go to an Hotel.

"Sir, can I be accommodated here?"

"Whom are you with?"

"No one but my family."

"No, we don't accommodate niggers here."

I go to another, "Can I get supper and lodgings here to night?"

"Yes, yes,—walk in."

The bell rings, I take my wife and children, and start for the tea room.

"Where are you going?"

"To supper, sir."

"We don't sit niggers down with white folks here."

We will suppose the next day Sunday. The church-bells are ringing, and the cold reception we have met with hath made my heart sick and my life a burthen. What say you if we go to church? It is agreed on. We enter. In going down the aisle I am politely touched on the shoulder—"There is a seat in that corner for niggers."

"Sir, my wife is a member of this sect, of good and regular standing in her own church. This being Communion-day, she wishes to be with you."

"Oh, yes, brother; well, she must come this afternoon; we are going to take it this forenoon—this afternoon we will give it to the niggers."

I will suppose one of my children dead. It has been christened in this church. I apply to the church for the privilege of burying my child in their ground.

"Oh no, that will never do; we cannot allow niggers to be buried with white folks."

Poor foolish man! Here your reign of tyranny is over. Can you prevent us from entering the kingdom of heaven or the gates of hell with white folks? You follow us to the grave with your prejudices, but you can go no further.

When asked why we are treated thus, the answer is, "They are an ignorant, degraded race." Why are we ignorant and degraded? Are not the avenues to knowledge closed against us, and we made to black your boots, scrape your chin, cook your food, and do the rest of your dirty work, or starve? Do we not see it everywhere staring us in the face, as plain as though it were written—"No admittance here for niggers." True, your demoralising and brutalising process for three hundred and thirty-three years is enough to have unfitted us for society, but are you still afraid to give us and our sons an equal chance with you and yours? Yes, you see as clear as that king whose knees smote together with fear, from the writing on the wall, that ignorance is the only hope of slavery, that to enlighten the slaves would be to liberate them.

ONE

The Death of Mrs. Hanablue, and the Sale of Her Slaves at Public Auction

Here they are, old and young, male and female, married and single, to be sold to the highest bidder. My father, who belonged to a Mrs. Knox, is now dead; and I have no one to look to for parental affection and advice save my grandmother, whose gray hairs and many years' service in the public-house did not excuse her from the auctioneer's hammer. But she was not without a friend. She placed some thirty years' savings of money in his hands to purchase her and her son. She had two other children, a son and a daughter, but they were owned by other parties.

They began to sell off the old slaves first, as rubbish; one very old man sold for one dollar; the old cook sold for 17 dollars; from that to 1,600 dollars, which was the price of a young man who was a carpenter.

Dr. Norcom, whose daughter owned my sister, bought me for a shop boy. It would be in vain for me to attempt to give a description of my feelings while standing under the auctioneer's hammer; I can safely say, such will not be the case again. The sale is over, and each slave moves slowly along to his new home—some in one direction, and some in another.

The man, to whom my grandmother trusted to do her business for her, acted very honourably. As soon as it could be done, after the sale, he procured her free papers and the bill of sale of her son, to show that he was her property by right of purchase. It may seem rather strange that my grandmother should hold her son a slave; but the law requires it. She must give security that she will never be any expense to the town or state before she can come in possession of her freedom. Her property in him is sufficient to satisfy the law; he can be sold at any minute to pay her debts, though it is not likely this will ever be the case; they have a snug home of their own, but their troubles are not yet at an end.

My uncle Joseph, who was owned by Mr. J. Collins, ran away about this time and got as far as New York, where he was seen and known by Mr. Skinner of Edenton, who had him taken and sent back to his master. He was lodged in gaol and put in heavy irons, where he remained for most of the winter and was then sold to go to New Orleans.

My uncle Mark, whom my grandmother had bought, was steward on board of a packet or vessel of some kind at that time, and some months after my uncle Joseph had been sold, my uncle Mark met him in New York. He had made his second escape. The vessel was about to sail and they had but little time to spend with each other, though my uncle Joseph told him he had not come there to stop. His intention was to get beyond the reach of the Stars and Stripes of America. Unwilling to trust his liberty any longer in the hands

of a professed Christian, he promised to seek safety among
the Turks. Since then we have not heard from him, but feel
satisfied that he is beyond the reach of slavery, which is the
greatest satisfaction that can be given to us, his friends. Since
that time both my uncle and myself have travelled a great
deal, and never failed to inquire after him whenever we saw
any one that we knew—that being the only hope we have of
hearing from him.

My grandmother's mind had scarcely got composed about
my uncle, before I began to be a source of trouble to her.
The older I grew the greater was my hatred to slavery, and
I could not conceal it. I had called Mrs. Hanablue mistress,
because I heard everybody about the house call her mistress;
but when I went to the doctor who bought me, I could not call
him master nor his wife mistress. They were members of Mrs.
Hanablue's family. I have always called him doctor, and his
wife Miss Mary; this they may not have noticed. The next to
master were the children. Some slaveholders will make their
slaves "Master" and "Miss" their children from the cradle; but
such was not the case with the doctor; his boys were not "mas-
tered" until they were 10 or 12 years old. But when they got it
from others, and expected it from me, I was not ready to do
it. I could not make myself believe that they had any right to
demand any such humiliation from me. They saw it and often
thumped me over the head for it. I used all possible means to
avoid calling them by name; whenever I had to address them
I would go right up to them—"Your father" or "your mother,"

as the case might be, "wants you." It was not long before they began to take notice of that, and would question me—"Want who?" said they. "You." "Who am I?" Here they got me in a corner. But I took a turnabout—sometimes I would "master" them, and at other times I would take a rap.

The old doctor was a tyrant, and his wife was no better. His children were chips off the same block, some a little larger than others.

Here my grandmother used to teach me a doctrine that I could not appreciate then though it was not without effect. How it was that we could love slaveholders and bear the yoke with patience I could not tell; but I must say, that I never saw anything in her, that I could construe into hatred towards anyone. I have seen her treat these very children that were growing up to kick me about, with as much kindness as though they were hers—in fact, they would always look for something good, whenever they went where she was. I could daily see her, practising that which she so much wanted to teach me—love and forgiveness; to love those who loved not me, and forgive those that ill-treated me—a principle though right and just in itself, yet it is all that poor nature can do, and she is often found too weak for that.

TWO

The Happy Family, or Practical Christianity

There are many acts of men that are called acts of Christianity; but the practical Christian need not tell the world what he is. He is known and felt by all around of a kindred spirit. The words from his lips affect the soul of man, as drops of water the drooping plant. Such I have seen in the Slave States, but they are like lilies among thorns. Having nothing around to reflect back their beauty, they seem to be unfit for this world, or the world unfit for them. Such was the case with the Rev. Mr. Carnes, and his family. They had lived in Alexandria previous to their coming to Edenton. Mrs. Carnes had no children of her own. They had a woman with several children, whose husband was free, but she and the children belonged to Mr. Carnes; but as well as I could learn no longer than they saw fit to stop. Though they belonged to different churches, there seemed to be that love and union which adorns the Christian, and commends him to the world.

The question about what Paul or Apollos preached did not disturb them; their chief study was their duty to God, and to man. Mrs. Carnes employed herself in teaching the children how to read and write. Her affection for the children, and theirs for her, in return, made her task a pleasant one. She was more like a mother than a mistress, so much so that their mother and father gave themselves no care about them farther than to keep them clean and neat, knowing that Mrs. Carnes would do more for them than they could possibly do. Mr. Carnes had not been there long before the degraded state in which he found the slaves everywhere around him attracted his attention; and seeing that some of the other sects had given the use of the church to the slaves at stated times for evil, he resolved to get the use of his church, if possible, for their good. It was agreed on by the members, that he could have the use of it every Sunday evening to preach to the slaves. At first, they cared but little to go and hear Mr. Carnes, thinking that no good could be gained by going to the brick church. It was known by this name to all the slaves, and the members were considered a congregation of tyrants; but Mr. Carnes had not preached many sermons before his congregation rapidly increased, and he was satisfied that they appreciated his labours of love. He also took great pleasure in explaining such passages of Scripture as they could not understand to all who would call at his house. The slaves occupied the pews; and their masters, if any of them came, occupied the gallery. His sermons in the evenings were extemporary, which was still more pleasing to the slaves. They look upon written sermons as being stale and dry, but there was nothing dry about these, they were animating and instructive. In the course of Mr. Carnes's labour among the slaves, he preached a series of sermons on the Lord's Prayer, which gave great satisfaction to his hearers. The slaveholders would come at times to hear whether he was preaching after the manner of their fathers—"Servants, obey your masters and mistresses;" or the seditious doctrine for which Paul was tried before Felix; or like the doctrine he preached to Philemon, his exhortations to brotherly love and Christian kindness. I mention this case of Onesimus, because it has been so frequently used to prove that Paul the Apostle was a slave-catcher; but let their opinion of Paul be what it may, they heard nothing here at Mr. Carnes's church that could be construed into anything but brotherly love and Christian fellowship. Indeed they thought there was too much of it, and began to complain, saying that Mr. Carnes took more interest in preaching to the niggers than he did to them. Several of them were quite displeased, but they had heard of nothing coming from his lips respecting their condition as slaves. He had laboured to enlighten and elevate them, saying nothing to create excitement among the slaves or their masters. To stop him from preaching to them without some better cause than they had as yet been able to find, while other Churches were allowing this privilege to their slaves, would look rather anti-Christian, and appearance is about all with them; but that good woman, Mrs. Carnes, had not been with us long before she left the field to receive of her father the reward for the few days she had laboured in his vineyard. This world seemed not her home, she was here to teach those little ones how to love and how to live, and above all how to die; then left them to mourn her loss not alone, but in common with all who knew her.

> In yon churchyard her body lies,
> Confined beneath the sod;
> Her spirit dwells beyond the skies,
> With its father—God.

How refreshing it is to the soul to call the past life of such spirits to mind. Though dead, they yet live in our memory, and often seem to rebuke us for our slothfulness and want of humanity. Whether they ever said anything to Mr. Carnes about his preaching or not I cannot say, but soon after the death of his wife he left Edenton for Alexandria, but with the satisfaction that he had done some good, and had not left a slave behind who knew him who did not believe him to be his friend.

I will give another case of a Christian character, which I think was partly caused by his influence. It was a widow lady; Mrs. Basill was her name; she owned some eight or ten slaves, left to her by her husband at his death. He was a sea-faring Captain, and being the most of his time from home, Mrs. Basill's life was rather a retired one. She was seldom seen from home, and after the death of her husband still less so. She was somewhat of a delicate constitution, and advanced in years. Not long after the death of Captain Basill she was taken to her bed, where she remained gradually sinking under her disease. At last finding her time of departure near at hand, and that it was necessary for her to see how things stood between her and Him before whom she would shortly have to stand, she had all her slaves called in to her room. After telling them all that she was about to leave them, but leaning on Him who was able to save, she was not without hope of a brighter world, she said—"I have given you that which I never had a right to withhold from you—your freedom. It is yours by nature." After having divided the most of the property among them, she called a very old woman to her—"Here is my rocking chair; you are old, and past labour; let your children and grandchildren wait on you, as you have waited on them, while you enjoy the little comfort that this world can afford; but let it not be the means of robbing you of the happiness that awaits us in the world to come." A few days more of suffering passed, and Mrs. Basill felt the last fond link of nature break and her captive soul set free. They all gathered around her dying bed with weeping eyes and throbbing hearts, to take their last farewell of one for whom a new spring of love had been opened in every bosom. This last act of her life had satisfied them that she was their friend, the greatest friend they had on earth, one with whom they were now loth to part, not knowing where to look for protection in time of need. Mrs. Basill, after this business had been attended to of freeing her slaves, took her leave of them all, asking each one to meet her in the promised land, where there would be no more sickness nor death, no more sorrowing and mourning, no more weeping around the beds of dying friends; but one continued hosannah to our King, who has given us the victory over death. With this last request she bade them all farewell, and left the world, I trust, for a better.

Mr. John Cox was one of the guardians for the slaves, I do not know any other, though I suppose there were others. Whether these poor slaves, which were all women and children, ever got all that their mistress left them or not, it is hard to say; but this much I know—they were talking of making slaves of them again before I left there. It is not the least unlikely that they are all slaves again long before this. The law is against them, it does not favour abolition. They are at the mercy of the people, and the people are without mercy.

THREE

Brutality and Murder among Slaves

I am not writing of what I have heard, but of what I have seen, and of what I defy the world to prove false. There lived about two miles up a river, emptying into the Albemarle Sound, a planter, whose name was Carbaras. His plantation was called Pembroke. At his death his slaves were sold. I mention this, because slaves seldom ever have more than one name; their surname is most generally that of their first master's. The person I am now about to allude to was known by the name of George Carbaras. After the death of his old master, he was owned by Mr. Popelston; after that by young John Horton, who sold him to a negro trader, whose name was Ham. I think this Mr. Ham was from Georgia.

George was chained in the gang with other slaves, and dragged from his wife and his friends. After a few days' travel on the road, by some means or other he made his escape and returned back to that spot where he knew he could find one heart to feel for him, in whom he could confide; but he had not been there long before the bloodthirsty negro-hunters got on his trail, one beautiful Sunday morning, about midsummer, while the church-bells were ringing.

Willy Ray, Elisha Besell, Rob Keaton and Tom Man were pulling up the Albemarle to murder a brother; this, no doubt, they did with fiendish relish. The next question with them was, whether the mere gratification of killing a man and cutting his head from his body was the only pay they were to receive or not.

"If he is outlawed, we only need show his head, and the reward is ours; but if he is not outlawed, what then? Why, they may try to make us pay for him; but we will not be fools enough to say that we shot him, unless we are to be paid for shooting him." His body is put into a canoe; his head thrown in, which lies on his breast. These four Southern gentlemen now return to the town, leaving the canoe to inquire how the advertisement reads. On finding that the reward was to be given to any one who would apprehend and confine him in any gaol in the State, they saw that they could not publicly boast of their fiendish work; but the Sunday following they brought him down for exhibition.

Now, the question is, what had this man done that he should be so inhumanly butchered and beheaded? The crime that he had committed, and the only crime, was to leave the unnatural trader in slaves and the souls of men, to return to his natural and affectionate wife. Nothing is done to the murderers. They only made a blunder. Slaves are outlawed and shot with impunity, and the tyrant that shoots them is paid for it; but in this case George was not outlawed, so their trouble was all for nothing, and the glory only known to themselves.

Tom Hoskins was a slave belonging to James Norcom, the

son of Dr. Norcom. This slave was found just out of the town
in the scrub, said to have been shot by William Ray. He was
shot in the back, and must have been killed instantly. There
was no pay for this—only a feast of blood. Tom's crime was
running away from one whom I know to be an unmerci-
ful tyrant. Another was shot, but not killed. Sirus Coffield—
There were three brothers of the Coffields, William, James,
and Josiah; I know not which of the three this slave belonged
to. They had been out that day with their bloodhounds hunt-
ing slaves. They shot Sirus a little before dark. By some means
or other he made his escape from them, and reached Dr. Sawyer's shop soon after dark. He was taken in, and as many of the
shots taken out of him as they could get at, and his wounds
dressed. This being done, Dr. Sawyer sent a despatch to Mr.
Coffield to let him know that the slave that they had shot
had come in to him, and got his wounds dressed. As soon as
they received this intelligence, they mounted their horses, and
rode off in fiendish glee for town. They came up to the shop,
hooting and yelling as if all Bedlam was coming. When they
had reached the door, the first cry from them was, "Bring him
out—finish him—I shot dat nigger—whenever I put my gun
at a nigger, he's boun' to fall." This man, who was taking so
much glory to himself, was not one of the Coffields. I would
give his name, but it is so nearly connected with the name of
one of Mr. Coffield's slaves, that I do not know which is his.
The doctor came out and said to them, "Gentlemen, the negro
has given himself up to me, and I will be responsible for his
safe delivery to you as soon as he is able to be moved from

here; but at present he is not." Seeing that the doctor would not let them have him they returned home.

The Coffields were very rich, they owned a great many slaves, and shooting with them was common. They did not feel the loss of a slave or two; it was a common thing for them to offer 50 or 100 dollars' reward for a slave, dead or alive, so that there be satisfactory proof of his having been killed. I came very near being torn to pieces one day by Coffield's bloodhounds. I was sent to my master's plantation with a message to the overseer; the plantation was about one and a half miles from town; I knew what part of it he had the slaves at work on, and took a short cut through the bush; when I had got in sight Coffield hallooed to me to keep off, and get over the fence, otherwise I should have them on me. He was then trying to strike the track of a slave. They have been hunted so much that they have learnt to baffle the hounds when they can get means; to cut and rub an onion on the bottom of the foot is one way, to sprinkle cayenne pepper in their track is another.

I could mention other slaves that have been shot to my knowledge, but why should I? If one has been shot, and the laws justify the shooting of that one, every slave in the States is liable to be shot.

> Your air with misery howls,
> The negro groans, the bloodhound growls;
> Like demons wild you take their flesh,
> And human rights beneath you crush.

FOUR

The Different Ways of Punishing Slaves

Just at the back of the courthouse and in front of the gaol is a whipping post, with stocks and pillory attached. The pillory is not intended for slaves, it is a place where they put men or women when they want to pelt them with rotten eggs; the platform of the pillory is about 8 feet from the ground, 6 or 8 feet square, with a post in the centre—having in the centre of it a board firmly placed 3 feet from the platform, with 3 half circles on each side—two for the wrist, and one for the neck—and a corresponding slide board to let down and fasten them in; the person who is in the pillory stands in a stooping position. The stocks are made on the same principle, the lower part being the groundwork; at each end is a large post with iron straps to fasten the hand in; they are about as high as one can well get their hands in the required manner; this is done to tighten the skin on the back, that the cowhide they flog with may cut the deeper into the flesh. Here I have seen men and women stripped and struck, from 15 to 100 and more. Some of them whose backs were cut to pieces were washed down with strong brine or brandy, this is done to increase pain.

But the most cruel torture is backing; the hands are crossed
and tied, then taken over the knees and pinned by running a
stick between the arms and legs, which tightens the skin and
renders the slave as helpless as a child. The backing paddle
is made of oak, about 1¼ inch thick, and 5 by 8 inches in
the blade, with about 12 inches of a handle. The blade is full
of small holes, which makes the punishment severer than it
would otherwise be. I have seen the flesh like a steak. Slaves
flogged in this way are unable to sit down for months. This
was Mr. Collins's favourite way of punishing slaves. Mr. Collins was a member of the ——— Church, and to a stranger
would seem to be a very kind-hearted, good man. Every slave
that met him would pull off his hat and make a polite bow,
which Mr. Collins would return. If he was a day or two from
home, when he returned, his slaves that were about the house,
would take his hand and inquire after his health. Is it love, that
his own and other people's slaves have for him? No, but fear.
Mr. Collins always has at hand a little cane, to teach politeness
to such as have not learnt it. I have known him to flog others'
slaves for not taking their hats off to him, when he has been
on the opposite side of the street; and on one occasion he met
a slave with a quarter of mutton in each hand, and flogged
him because he did not shift the two into one hand, until he
could raise his hat. Where the slaves cannot see the necessity
of being deceitful, such treatment soon makes them see it.

I was an eye-witness to more than one hundred blows each,
being given to two lads belonging to Mr. Collins, and they

were then sent to the Lake Farm, a place that will well bear the name I once heard a poor slave mother call it, who was taking leave of her son—"He is going," said she, "to the lake of hell."

I will give you but one more case of flogging detail, that will be Agnes, the slave of Augustus Moore. She was hired to John Beasley; she was some six months advanced in pregnancy at the time. Being in an unfit state for field labour, she could not do as much as other slaves. For this cause, Beasley tied her up and commenced whipping her. With my own hands have I dressed her back, and I declare, before God, that she had not a piece of skin left on it as wide as my finger. She was a hired slave. If Beasley had killed her at a single blow, her master could have punished Beasley if he could have got white witnesses to that effect, which is not likely; but she may have died in an hour after being cut down, and there was no law to harm him. It would have been death caused by moderate correction, which North Carolina does not punish a slaveholder for.

I know that the picture I have drawn of slavery is a black one, and looks most unnatural; but here you have the State, the town, and the names of all the parties. Prove it to be false if you can. Take one who has never felt the sting of slavery, he would naturally suppose that it was to the slaveholder's advantage to treat his slaves with kindness; but the more indulgent the master, the more intelligent the slave; the more intelligent the slave, the nearer he approximates to a man; the nearer he approximates to a man, the more determinate he is to be a free man; and to argue that the slaves are happy, or can be happy while in slavery, is to argue that they have been brutalised to that degree that they cannot be considered men. What better proof do you want in favour of universal freedom that can be given? You can find thousands of ignorant men who will lay down their lives for their liberty; can you find one intelligent man that would prefer slavery? These thousands are not men—they are only children to what they should be. I am yet a child; I can see the things that I want, but have not attained to the stature of a man; they are beyond my reach, though I would be ashamed of myself to offer these acts of wanton cruelty as a reason why slavery should be abolished. If they can be considered an evil, they are a necessary evil, and you can only remove the evil by removing the cause. All the chains and fetters in North Carolina would not hold me if I was able to carry them off. God created me a freeman and with His assistance I will die one. If any man has a right to my limbs, he also has a right to use all necessary means to make them available to him. I deny the former; and declare it as an act of Christian duty, in regard to the latter, that the slaveholder who gets my labour shall pay as much as it is worth for it, and his life, if possible, with it.

The last thing that remained to be done to complete this hell on earth was done in 1850 in passing the Fugitive Slave Law. There is not a State, a city, nor a town left as a refuge for the hunted slave; there is not a United States officer but

what has sworn to act the part of the bloodhound in hunt-
ing me down, if I dare visit the land of Stars and Stripes, the
home of the brave, and land of the free. You can extort sub-
mission to the gratification of your lust from our wives—you
can take our daughters, and sell them for the basest use that
can be made of woman. Yet you declare it to be a self-evident
truth that all men are created by their Creator free and equal,
and endowed with certain inalienable rights—life, liberty, and
the pursuit of happiness. Where are the coloured man's rights
to-day in America? They once had rights allowed them. Yes,
in the days that tried men's souls, they had a right to bleed
and die for the country; but their deeds are forgotten, their
swords and bayonets have been beaten into chains and fetters
to bind the limbs of their children. To your shame and dis-
grace, the first man that was seen to fall in the city of Boston,
in the revolutionary struggle for liberty, was a coloured man;
and I have seen one of his brethren, who had fled from his
whips and chains, within sight of that monument erected to
liberty, dragged from it into slavery, not by the slaveowners
of the south, for they knew not of his being there—but by
northern men.

FIVE

My Sister Has Run Away, My Aunt, Two Children, and Myself Sent to Gaol

Here I am! looking through the grates of your prison. What have I done? What has my aunt done? What could those little children do? We are not accused of anything.

The old doctor, no doubt, thought that this would be the means of bringing my sister back; but you will by-and-by see, that she did not leave with the intention of returning. She had not yet been called to make her back bare for the lash; but she had gone to live on the doctor's plantation, where she daily expected it. Her mental sufferings were more than she could longer bear. With her it was, in the language of one of our fathers, "liberty or death."

The doctor offers 100 dollars reward for her, and threatens to punish to the extreme penalty of the law, any person or persons found harbouring, or assisting her in any way to make her escape. He then wrote a letter to a gentleman living in New York, who had formerly lived in North Carolina, by the name of Tredwill. I am not prepared to say that Mr. Tredwill took an interest in this letter. I rather believe he did not. But the news was soon circulated among the slave catchers of the north, and they were sticking their unwanted faces in every coloured man's door, on account of my sister. The doctor pretended to sell me and the two children to a negro trader. In two or three weeks he received a letter from New York, stating that my sister was taken, and safe lodged in gaol. This calls the old man from home. He has got to prove property and pay expenses. Now that the old doctor is gone, I am having a jolly good time. Mr. Lamb, the jailer, was an old acquaintance of mine. Though he was a white man, and I a slave, we had spent many hours together in Mr. Johnson's family. We had taken tea there. To make my story short, and go back to the doctor, Mr. Johnson had a very fine daughter, and we were very fond of each other. Mr. Lamb had been a visitor of Mr. Johnson's for many years. Now that he had me under the lock and key, knowing that it was not for any crime that I was there, he could not be otherwise than kind. He allowed me every indulgence. My friends could call and see me whenever they pleased, such as could come, and stop as long as they liked; he would never turn the key on them. Sometimes he would give me the key on the inside. While the doctor had me here for safe keeping, I could have made my escape every day or night; but in the first place, if I had wanted to go, I would not have taken the advantage of Mr. Lamb's kindness; in the second place, I saw no chance of bettering myself. I knew he would not get my sister, because she had not left town. My uncle-in-law, who was a seafaring man, had intended to take her to New York, but the doctor's threats frightened him so, that he did not dare make the attempt.

While the old man was gone I had a negro trader call with others to see me. His name was Gaskins; he said he would buy me if the old doctor would sell me; I told him I thought he would—that he told me he intended to do so when he put me in.

After some two weeks the doctor returns home without my sister. The woman that had been taken up and put in gaol was a free woman, but what could she do with the wretch who put her there. America is a free country and a white man can do what he pleases with a coloured man or woman in most of the States. They may have a few friends now who would not allow this if they knew it; but they are hated by the nation at large who do it.

My aunt is taken out of gaol and sent home to the doctor's house, the children and myself are left in. The old man comes to have a little talk with me about my sister.

"Well, John, I have not got Harriet yet, but I will have her yet. Don't you know where she is?"

"How can I know, sir? I have been in gaol ever since my sister left you. Mr. Gaskins was here while you were away, sir, and said that he wanted to buy me."

"Buy you! I don't want to sell you."

"You told me when you put me here that you did."

"Yes, but not if you will go back to the shop and behave yourself. Mr. Gaskins has not got money enough to buy you."

"I do not know how to behave differently from what I have done."

"Your behaviour will do; but I am afraid you are going to run away from me."

"I have not said anything about running away from you, sir."

"I know that; but your sister is gone, and you will be going next."

With this we parted. About this time my uncle-in-law returns. The doctor forbid his going to see my aunt. Her husband was owned by another man. They had lived together for twenty years, and I had never heard them quarrel; and now they are to be separated, not for anything they had done, but for the acts of another. But such are the laws and customs of the country; and as hard as it is, yet we must bear it; there is no help for us. My uncle-in-law's name was Stephen. His master, Mr. Bozman, was owner of the vessel he sailed in, and though he had several chances to make his escape from slavery, yet he had returned on every voyage. What was next to his liberty to him was that in slavery his wife was with him. When that union between him and her was broken, the charm of slavery was lost, and he returned no more. His wife to him was dead—ay, worse than dead; he could see her living spirit, but dare not approach it. "That which God hath joined together, let no man put asunder," saith the Scriptures.

At the doctor's last visit to the gaol, he laid before me the wretchedness of the free people of colour in New York, stating that they had not the comforts of his slaves and how much better off we were than they. To this I said nothing. My mind was fully made up on this subject—first, that I must, in order to effect my escape, hide as much as possible my hatred to slavery, and affect a love for my master, whoever he might be; the doctor and myself knew each other too well for me to hope to better my condition with him; I must change hands in order to do that. Secondly, let the condition of the coloured people of New York be what it may, I had rather die a free man than live a slave. The doctor evidently does not want to sell me, neither does he want to run any risk of losing me; neither was it from any particular fondness that he had for me; it was that he could not replace me for the same money that a trader would give for me. Before he left the gaol he told me that he did not want to keep me in gaol any longer, and would let me out at any time when I would get my uncle Marcus to stand my security that I would not run away from him. When leaving, he told me to send for my uncle and see if he would not do it for me. To all this I was dumb. I was in no particular hurry to get out of gaol. I wanted a little serious reflection, and here was the only place where I could get an opportunity of the kind.

A few days passed, and he heard nothing from me. He saw my uncle and told him that I wanted to see him at the gaol. He accordingly came and asked me if I wanted him to stand my security. I promptly told him no; that I wanted my liberty, and I would make good the first opportunity to get it; that he might do as he pleased, but God being my helper I would die a free man. This satisfied my uncle at once that he had as well take the money out of his pocket, and pay for me, as to stand my security, and if I could get a chance to make my escape without bringing any expense on him so much the better. Here we parted. The old doctor waits for an answer, but gets none, which satisfied him that I no longer had a desire to make his shop my home.

There were two or three slaveholders in the town that would give him more for me than he could get from a trader, but he would not sell me to any one in the town. Mr. Sawyer, who afterwards bought me, came to the gaol, and asked me if I would live with him, if he bought me. I told him that I would, but the question was not asked how long.

I had been here just two months when Mr. Sawyer got a negro trader, whose name was Law, to buy the two children for my grandmother and one for himself. The doctor at first tried to bind the trader not to sell me to any one in the State, but this he would not agree to, saying, he sold his slaves where ever he could get the most for them—he finally agreed to take me out of town in irons, but to sell me the first chance he could get. The old man did not think that he had bargained for me before I was sold. This important part of the business being settled we were sold, the two children for 500 dollars, I believe, and I for 900 dollars. Now for the remnant of our father's old bayonets in the shape of handcuffs; the blacksmith's tools, handcuffs and chain are all in readiness at the gaol. The chain is 30 or 40 feet long, with handcuffs every two or three feet. The slaves are handcuffed right and left on each side of the chain. In the gang there was one who was free by birth. He was born not more than fifty miles from Edenton. He had been put in gaol here for some trifling offence; not being able to pay the fine he was sold for six months or a year to William Roberts, a planter, who was so cruel to him that he ran away from him. He was caught, and after being flogged, was put in irons and set to work. He attempted to cut the irons off, and was caught in the act, sent to gaol, and finally sold to a trader. I saw the irons that he had been made to work in, they were fetters for the ankles, weighing from 15 to 20 pounds in weight.

Now we are all snugly chained up, the children in the cart, and the women walking behind; your friend weeping and taking a farewell shake of the hand with you; wives of their husbands, and parents of their children. I went with the gang as far as Mr. J. B. Skinner's, the man that had my uncle taken in New York. Here the cart was stopped and the blacksmith's tools taken out, and Mr. Law began to hammer away at my irons. When they were off he told me to take the children and go home to Mr. Sawyer; the children went to my grandmother, and I to Mr. Sawyer, not the dealer in sausage meat, but S. T. Sawyer of North Carolina. I make this explanation, because they were both members of Congress.

SIX

My Fifth and Last Master

By this time I had seen enough of slavery to make my life bitter, but I had resolved to hide it if possible. When I met Mr. Sawyer I saluted him as my master. It came rather hard to me at first to "master" a man, and act the deceitful part of a slave, to pretend love and friendship where I had none. As unpleasant as it was thus to act, yet under the circumstances in which I was placed, I feel that I have done no wrong in so doing; I did everything that I could to please my present master, who treated me with as much kindness as I could expect from any one to whom I was a slave. He had a brother, Dr. M. E. Sawyer, who was subject to fits. My master was a lawyer, my business was to wait on the lawyer and take care of his brother when sick. Sometimes when recovering from his fits he would be perfectly mad for four or five days. On such occasions I visited the sick slaves on the plantation. This part of my work caused the overseer a great deal of unpleasantness; he would sometimes want to give them oil or something of the kind, saying they were not sick; at other times he would say they were well enough to go to work, and if they were too sick to work, they were too sick to eat. Knowing that he would not strike me for having my own way in what I was sent there for—to see if they were sick and give them what they needed—I took great pleasure in differing with him on all occasions whenever I thought my patient dangerously ill. If Dr. Sawyer was not in his right mind I would call in Dr. Warren. My judgment in regard to such diseases as are most common on a plantation was considered very good for one of my age; so much so, that a young planter who was studying medicine at the time offered my master one thousand five-hundred dollars for me. The way I came to know this was this: he asked me one day if I wanted to be sold. This woke up a little of the old feeling, and I had almost forgot myself for a minute.

"No sir," I said, "I am not anxious to be sold, but I know I have got to serve some one." Here he made me a promise which I shall never forget, though it was not consoling to me. He said, "you shall not serve any one after me, I have been offered a handsome price for you; but I don't want to sell you." True, I was glad to hear him say that I would serve no one after him; this required a little consideration; he was but a few years older than me, and to wait for him to die looked to me too much like giving a man who was in want of his daily bread a cheque on the bank to be paid when he is dead. To have prayed for his death would have been unkind; to have killed him would have been worse; so finally I concluded to let him live as long as the Lord was willing he should, and I would get rid of him, as soon as possible. My pride would

not allow me to let a man feed and clothe me for nothing,
I would work the ends of my fingers off first.

I have said nothing about Mr. Sawyer's plantation slaves;
I have only spoken of his treatment to me. I am willing to
acknowledge kindness even in a slaveholder wherever I have
seen it; but had he treated all of his slaves as he treated me,
the probability is that they would have been of as little value
to him as I was. Some might try to make out a case of ingrat-
itude of this, but I do not feel myself under the slightest obli-
gation to any one who holds me against my will, though he
starved himself to feast me. Doubtless he meant to do me a
good turn; but he put it off too far.

I must drop Mr. Sawyer for a few minutes, the Doctor is
not satisfied yet. He has had my uncle arrested, and lodged
in gaol; I too am an eyesore to him; the first time that I met
him after he sold me, he stopped me. I had crossed the street
twice to avoid him, but in vain. He told me to stop. I replied
that I was on an errand and could not stop. He insisted on my
stopping. I did so, but some distance off. He began very calmly
to ask me several questions about my sister, to which I gave no
satisfactory answer; finally, he got in such a rage I thought it
best to leave. The last words I heard from him were—"I will
butcher you, you. . . . ."

In the evening I went to see my uncle at the gaol. I was
obliged to pass by the Doctor's shop doors, or go round a square
out of my way. He saw me when I passed. I was on the look-out
all the while at the gaol for him, and on my return he had taken
his stand in the tavern, between his shop and the gaol. When

I got abreast of him, he made a bolt for me, and I made one
from him. We had quite a foot race for two or three hundred
yards. The old doctor, finding his legs, though longer, not quite
as supple as mine, gave up the chase. This may be all imagina-
tion, but I had made a study of the old doctor's ways so long that
I really thought I could sometimes tell what he was thinking
about. Whether I could or not, I baffled him four times when he
had thought to catch me. It was near two years before the doctor
could let me pass him without giving me a look that meant anything but friendship. He sees my grandmother has some friend,
and takes my uncle out of gaol for trial. The only charge that he
could bring against him was that he was going about looking
like a gentleman, having as much money as he had. The Court
said, that unless the doctor could prove that he came dishon-
estly by this money, they could not find him guilty of any crime;
and yet my grandmother had to pay the expense of the Court.

Here the doctor seemed to give up all further intentions of
trying to revenge himself on us for what my sister had done.
Three long years are passed and gone, and my sister not yet
free. She is still within five miles of the spot where she was
born, seeing her master almost every day through the cracks
of her place of concealment.

> Dark and gloomy is the captive's cell,
> No light of day e'er enters there;
> The feelings of a broken heart no one can tell;
> It sickens, it weakens, it sinks in despair.

SEVEN

Dr. Sawyer's Death—His Brother's Election to Congress—and Marriage— and My Escape from Him

My master, after being elected, sent his brother to the plantation, to remain there until he returned from Washington. He had been there but a few days before he had a fit. In the morning, while dressing, he had gone to the fire to warm his hands; while there, and alone, the fit came on him; he fell in the fire, and remained there until the fit was over. He had got out of the fire before he was seen by any one; the first to see him was one of the women, who gave the alarm. The overseer sent a slave in haste for his brother and the doctor. I then took the horse, and after getting such things as were necessary, I was on the spot as soon as possible. One of his arms was completely baked. When I went up to his bed, he looked up and said, "It is too late; I am beyond all cure," though he allowed me to go on as I had begun, applying a little oil to some burns on his neck, while other arrangements were being made previous to the arrival of the doctor, who soon came and dressed his wounds. The doctor told my master that his brother could not live—that his case was an incurable one; and that death must soon follow. His brother and myself stopped with him until he died. He lived twelve or fifteen hours. At the remark that he made when I first went to his bed, before the doctor or his brother had arrived, I could not help from weeping. This was a sad accident; but no blame could be attached to any one. His brother had been like a father to him.

This misfortune being over, I am ordered to get ready for Washington City; this being done, we start off on our journey. We were not many days getting to this place, that I so much wanted to see. At the head of Pennsylvania Avenue, a little on the hill, is seen the capital of the United States—the place where they make laws for a nation of freemen. Down the Avenue a little, and on the left-hand side, is the slave-pen where they fat Americans for the market. The upper crust of the place consists principally of woman-whippers, blacklegs, blackguards, and dough faces. If a lady comes and rings the doorbell, and you, on answering it, tell her that the mistress is not in, the reply most invariably is, "Go and tell her who it is, and she will be in." Just as well say, "Go and tell her she has lied, not knowing who has called to see her." The same is the case of the gentlemen. Here is a bill before the House that they have spent weeks in discussing its merits and demerits; it is now to be voted on at such an hour. The sergeant-at-arms is sent out in search of the absent members; some of them are having a little game of cards—could not think of waiting until after 4 o'clock; the pay is just the same for playing cards as though they were making laws, only you must lie a little when the sergeant-at-arms calls, and say that you are not in.

I could not bear this system of lying. I avoided answering these calls whenever I could.

Here I had a chance of seeing some of the great men of the country. Mr. Van Buren, the bloodhound importer, and Henry Clay, the great polka [poker] player. He was a man of extraordinary talent; well understood public opinion; never helped to make it, but went with it; Dan Webster, one of the master-workmen on the Fugitive Slave Bill, was there; Graves, the butcher, was there; and the Honorable John Q. Adams was there, attending to his business.

After my master had been there a short time he went to board with Mrs. Payton, who had two young nieces here. He got over head and ears in love, and soon they were engaged to be married. As good luck would have it, this young lady had a sister living in Chicago, and no place would suit her like that to get married in. I admired her taste much. I wanted to go there too. My master could not do otherwise than give his consent to go there with her. The next question to be settled was about taking me with him into a free State. Near the time for him to leave, he told me that he intended to marry. I was pleased at this, and anxious to know who the fortunate lady might be. He did not hesitate to tell me what he intended to do, stating at the same time that he would take me with him if I would not leave him. "Sir," said I, "I never thought before that you suspected me of wanting to leave you."

"I do not suspect you, John. Some of the members of the House have tried to make me believe that you would run away if I took you with me; but my belief of you is that you would follow me to ——— and back."

"Well, sir, I would follow you back, sure, but if I could get out of the job of going there with you, I rather think I should."

"Well! get my things all ready; we are to leave on the first day of next week, I will try you anyhow."

Everything was ready, and the hoped-for time came. He took his intended, and off we started for the West. When we were taking the boat at Baltimore for Philadelphia, he came up to me and said, "Call me Mr. Sawyer, and if any body asks you who you are, and where you are going, do you tell them that you are a free man, and hired by me." This I agreed to do with all my heart.

We stopped two or three days at the Niagara Falls; from thence we went to Buffalo, and took the boat for Chicago; Mr. Sawyer had been here but a few days before he was taken sick. In five weeks from the time of his arrival here he was married, and ready to leave for home. On our return we went into Canada. Here I wanted to leave him, but there was my sister and a friend of mine at home in slavery; I had succeeded in getting papers that might have been of great value to my friend. I had tried, but could not get anything to answer my purpose. I tried to get a seaman's protection from the English Custom House, but could not without swearing to a lie, which I did not feel disposed to do.

We left here for New York, where we stopped three or four days. I went to see some of my old friends from home, who I knew were living there. I told them that I wanted their advice. They knew me, they knew my master, and they knew my friends also. "Now tell me my duty," said I. The answer was a very natural one—"look out for yourself first."

I weighed the matter in my mind, and found the balance in favour of stopping. If I returned I could do my sister no good, and could see no further chance for my own escape. I then set myself to work to get my clothes out of the Astor House hotel, where we were stopping; I brought them out in small parcels, as if to be washed. This job being done, the next thing was to get my trunks to put them in. I went to Mr. Johnson's shop, which was in sight of the Astor House hotel, and told him that I wanted to get my trunk repaired. The next morning I took my trunk in my hand with me; when I went down, whom should I see at the foot of the steps but Mr. Sawyer. I walked up to him, and I showed him a rip in the top of the trunk, opening it at the same time that he might see that I was not running off. He told me that I could change it, or get a new one if I liked. I thanked him, and told him we were very near home now, and with a little repair the old one would do. At this we parted. I got a friend to call and get my trunk, and pack up my things for me, that I might be able to get them at any minute. Mr. Sawyer told me to get everything of his in, and be ready to leave for home the next day. I went to all the places where I had carried anything of his, and where they were not done, I got their cards and left word for them to be ready by the next morning. What I had got were packed in his trunk; what I had not been able to get, there were the cards for them in his room. They dine at the Astor at 3 o'clock—they leave the room at 4 o'clock, at half-past 4 I am to be on the board of the boat for Providence. Being unable to write myself at that time, and unwilling to leave him in suspense, I got a friend to write as follows:—

"Sir—I have left you not to return; when I have got settled I will give you further satisfaction. No longer yours, John S. Jacob [*sic*]."

This note was to be put into the post-office in time for him to get it the next morning; I waited on him and his wife at dinner. As the town clock struck four I left the room. I then went through to New Bedford, where I stopped for a few months.

There were some things connected with my leaving which caused me a very unpleasant feeling. In the first place, he trusted me with anything and everything; his money and, I might say, his life. In the second place, he was willing that I should enjoy life a little, if there can be any for a slave. I have come off without bidding him farewell, without telling him where I am going, or why I go. I have got his pistols with me, that I have carried north and south. A robber, some would say, but stay a little; let us see how far I am a robber. The law of the land says that I am Mr. Sawyer's property. When I left New York I did not know but this piece of property of my master's might be disturbed by someone. I had taken the pistols for its protection. But if I had had the money to have bought others I never would have brought his away. I do not wish to be understood to blame slaves, under ordinary circumstances, for taking anything that they want and can get from their masters. I would take it, and thank God for the chance. But where a man is denied nothing, and entrusted with everything—denied nothing, did I say? He is denied the only thing that could justify him in betraying such trust, that is his liberty, the fountain of all our joy, without which we are the most miserable of all created beings.

Thank God! I am now out of their reach, the old doctor is dead; I can forgive him for what he did do, and would have done if he could. The lawyer I have quite a friendly feeling for, and would be pleased to meet him as a countryman and a brother, but not as a master. Though my mental sufferings had become such that it made life a burthen to me, yet I bear but one scar from the hand of my oppressors, and that not unrevenged.

EIGHT

My Voyage to the South Seas, and the Object of the Voyage— My Sister's Escape, and Our Meeting

The first thing that I strove to do was to raise myself up above the level of the beast, where slavery had left me, and fit myself for the society of man. I first tried this in New Bedford by working in the day and going to school at nights. Sometimes my business would be such that I could not attend evening schools; so I thought the better plan would be to get such books as I would want, and go a voyage to sea. I accordingly shipped on board the *Frances Henrietta*, of New Bedford.

This was a whaling voyage, but I will not trouble you with any fishing stories. I will make it short. After being absent three years and a half we returned home with a full ship, 1700 barrels of sperm oil and 1400 whale oil.

I had made the best possible use of my leisure hours on board, and kept the object that drove me from my friends and my home before me when on shore. I had promised myself if what money I had coming to me would be an inducement to any one to bring my sister off from the south, I would have her; but there was better news than that, in the bosom of an old friend, waiting to be delivered. The ship dropped her anchor, and the shore boats came off with friends of different persons on board, among whom was R. Piper. He had scarcely spoken to me before he began to tell me about my sister; her going to New Bedford in search of me, and her going back to New York, where, he told me, I should find her. This news to me was quite unexpected. I said, if my sister was free from her oppressor, I was a happy man. I hurried on shore, drew some money of the owners, and made my way to New York. I found my sister living with a respectable family as nurse at the Astor House. At first she did not look natural to me, but how should she look natural after having been shut out from the light of heaven for six years and eleven months; the most of this time spent in a place not more than three feet six inches in height! I did not wish to know what her sufferings were, while living in her place of concealment. The change that it had made in her, was enough to make one's soul cry out against this curse of curses, that has so long trampled humanity in the dust. She had in her possession two letters from the south, one written by the old doctor to Mr. Tredwill, who was then living in New York. After my sister had made her escape from the south, Mrs. Tredwill gave her this letter, that she might see what the doctor's feelings were. I am sorry that I have not got the letter, that it might be copied in this little narrative; when William Lloyd Garrison was about to leave the States for Europe on an anti-slavery mission, the coloured people of Boston met and passed some resolutions bearing testimony to their confidence in him as the uncompromising friend of the slave.

I gave him this letter at the same time, and told him that he could use it for the good of the cause. It was read several times, and published once or twice. In the letter the doctor offers 100 dollars reward for my sister, and after giving a description of her, he says—"I want to get her, to make an example of, for the good of the institution." The other letter was written by Caspar W. Norcom, a son of the old doctor. He tells my sister that if the family ever had entertained anything differing from a friendly feeling, that it no longer existed; they would be glad to see her once more happy at her old home with her friends around her.

Harriet, doubtless before this you have heard of the death of your Aunt Betty. Around her dying bed we all poured forth our tears in one common stream. She was a member of Mr. Johnson's Church. Oh, too high the price of knowledge! In her life she taught us how to live, and in her death she taught us how to die. This was the aunt of mine they so cruelly separated from her husband. My sister, while in the south, was secreted by a lady who is still living there, which prevents me from giving many of the facts of her confinement.

Miss Mary Matilda Norcom, to whom my sister had been given, got married to a northern man, whose name was Mesmore. He knew that my sister had been living in New York, and also knew the name of a young man there who knew my sister. He wrote a letter to this Mr. Burke offering to pay him for any information that he could give him that would enable him to get her. It was but a short time after this that I saw Mr. Burke in New York. He showed me the letter. I asked him if he would allow me to answer it. He said I might. I was then living in Boston. It was before Daniel Webster had assisted in making it a penal offence for a Christian to give a crust of bread, or shelter from the bitter blast, to the perishing traveller. I told him where and when he could find her, but he did not make me a call.

This unparalleled demonstration of American liberty and brotherly love was just being felt among the people of colour when I was about to leave the land of the free and home of the brave, for fear of being kidnapped. Mrs. W. sent for me to her room, and gave me her word that if I would be satisfied in leaving my sister with her she should not be carried off by any slaveholder. Feeling somewhat indignant at the idea of their coming, she said, "No, I will stop them myself at the door with a pistol first."

"Mrs. W.," said I, "I do not doubt your resolution; but how do you think you would act when it became necessary to fire?"

"I think I have nerve enough to do it," she replied.

But thanks to God it never came to this. The fleshmongers came, but they were not allowed to see her until she had been bought and paid for. Six years and eleven months she had been shut in in a cage; eight years after her escape from that she is hunted by the newly-manufactured bloodhounds of the north, and her friends made to pay 300 dollars to save her from being made the example spoken of in the doctor's letter.

The whole country was scoured from one end to the other. The southern planter would find his slave, and say to the northern man, "Go you and seize him;" and he dare not refuse.

NINE

The Laws of the United States respecting Slavery

In the original Constitution the word "slave" cannot be found; but it was well known by the nation that it was there, and that it was not in the power of Congress to wipe it out. In 1848, the Congress of the United States ordered a revised edition of the Constitution. First, I will give you a copy of the Declaration of Independence.

"We, the people of the United States, in order to form a more perfect union, establish justice, insure domestic tranquillity, provide for the common defence, promote the general welfare, and secure the blessings of liberty to ourselves and our posterity, do ordain and establish this Constitution for the United States of America."

I believe Henry Clay is as good an authority as I can find for the introduction of slavery into the United States, which was at that time one of the British colonies. At least, he has said as much against slavery and done as little for liberty as any man. If his statements are correct, slavery must have been introduced into the States in 1522, two hundred and sixty-five years before the adoption of the Constitution of the United States.

In 1791, four years after the adoption of the Constitution, the census of the States, as given in Hildreth's *History of the United States*, sets the Slaves down at. 697,697

In 1802, 11 years after, they had increased to 896,749

An increase of. 199,052

The present number is supposed to be 3,000,000

A still greater increase of. 2,103,251

In the infancy of their independence they passed a law in the United States Congress allowing the slave trade to be carried on between the United States and Africa for twenty years. This of itself was not sufficient for the slave-breeding part of this body of statesmen; they looked on abolition as a growing evil; they wanted a guarantee that slavery should not be touched in limb or branch until the twenty years had passed. In order to do this, they passed the following Act:—"Section 9.— The migration or importation of such persons as any of the States now existing shall think proper to admit shall not be prohibited by the Congress prior to the year One thousand eight hundred and eight; but a tax or duty may be imposed on such importation not exceeding ten dollars for each person."

How they do try to hide their infamy from the world! The mere passing of a law, of itself, does not seem so odious, though it be ever so unjust, if left open to the power that made it to amend it; but such is not the case in the law copied above. This ninth section, taken in connection with others of the same character, can have but one common-sense construction given to it, and that is—"We, the representatives of the people of the United States, here assembled this 17th day of September, A.D. 1787, do acknowledge the rights and guarantee protection to all such as may hereafter engage in the slave-trade between the United States and the coast of Africa. We further agree that no law passed by the Congress of the U.S. prior to 1808, can stop or check this trade in slaves and the souls of men." Yet the fleshmongers are not satisfied. They look to their numbers, and the number of their victims, and find themselves in the minority. They remember the blood that had just been spilt by their fathers about some tea, a little paper, and such-like things, which the more they were contrasted with the wrongs of the slave, the more insignificant they grew. They call on Congress not to protect the property, but to protect them against the evil that must and will, as sure as God rules the earth, grow out of it. It was given:— "Section 4, the United States shall guarantee to every State in this Union a republican form of government, and shall protect each of them against invasion, and on application of the Legislature or of the Executive (when the Legislature cannot be convened) against domestic violence."

Here is another piece of northern recreancy. Though many of them had opposed the slave trade, and some of them were trying to get rid of it in their own State, yet they would let every Bill that was brought before the House for the support of slavery become the law of the land. There is another Bill connected with others, as if to hide it, which is very necessary to complete this peculiar institution—it is a part of the 2nd section—"No person held to service or labour in one State, under the laws there, if escaping into another, shall, in consequence of any law or regulation therein, be discharged from such service or labour, but shall be delivered up on claim of the party to whom such service or labour may be due."

This law has direct reference to fugitive slaves, and no other class of persons; that law was not amended until 1850, when Daniel Webster and H. Clay, after a long struggle in Congress, finally succeeded in passing the amendment, which was the Fugitive Slave Law.

Now, my countrymen, for such you are, show me if you can, since the days of Adam, anything in which the laws of God and of nature, and the cries of humanity, were ever so little regarded as they were in that Bill; there was weeping and mourning from one end of the land to the other. All who could not be dragged into slavery—whether white or black, rich or poor, male or female—were threatened to be fined or imprisoned if they dared to give shelter, bread, water, or any aid whatsoever to the hunted slave. Every man in the United States employ was obliged to give his assistance when called on by the slave-hunters, and those who were not employed were made to honour and respect the law as the supreme law of the country. What says Isaiah x. 1, 2? "Woe unto them that decree unrighteous decrees; and that write grievousness which they have prescribed, to turn aside the needy from judgment, and to take away the right from the poor of my people, so that widows may be their prey, and that they may rob the fatherless." And, Isaiah lviii. 2–6, 7, "Yet they seek me daily, and delight to know my ways, as a nation that did righteousness, and forsook not the ordinances of their God; they ask of me the ordinances of Justice, they take delight in approaching to God. Is not this the fast that I have chosen, to loose the bands of wickedness, to undo the heavy burdens, and to let the oppressed go free, and that ye break every yoke? Is it not to deal thy bread to the hungry, and that thou bring the poor that are cast out to thy house; when thou seest the naked, that thou cover him, and that thou hide not thyself from thine own flesh?"

There are the laws of the United States, forbidding the nation to do a single act of humanity toward the most helpless and most needy known to man; here are God's laws, every one of which are written on our own hearts. And a man may as well attempt to deny his existence, as to deny his conviction of the rights of man, and the duty we owe to each other. But another word, from the Acts of the Apostles, iv. 19, "Whether it be right in the sight of God, to hearken unto man more than unto God, judge ye." This institution thinks there is nothing too holy to be made subservient to it. There is nothing in the catalogue of crime but what can be found in this unnatural hell on earth. The slave's life is a lingering death. The last glimmer of hope that cheered their sinking soul is gone. Their backs lacerated and bleeding; their limbs galled with chains and fetters; fleeing from slavery, when hunger and thirst compels them to stop; they see before them a large city; they see churches, hear the bells ringing, and see the people going in. They hear them call on God, and ask him to visit the sick and afflicted, the poor and the needy, and the distressed everywhere. The people all go home to enjoy the blessings of this life, so bountifully bestowed by their heavenly father, upon whom they have so lately called. The slaves drag along after them, and enter as Lazarus entered the rich man's premises. "Who are you, and what is your business here?"

"We have fled from the prison-house of bondage, and ask protection from the bands of our pursuers."

"Then you are runaway slaves?"

"We are, and ask your sympathy in the name of Him who tells us to remember those that are in bonds as being bound with them."

"Well, we do remember you all; we pray for you sometimes. What more can we do?"

"Sir, do we not owe certain duties to each other as men and brethren?"

"Yes, but I owe duties to your masters as well as you."

The one is an act of justice and mercy required by a just and merciful God; the other is not an injunction, but an unnatural prevention of the free exercise of your own conscience, in the elevation of bleeding humanity, whose sighs and groans have rent the air of heaven and sickened the soul of man. Hear Matthew xxvi. 42, 43, 44, "For I was an hungered, and ye gave me no meat. I was thirsty, and ye gave me no drink. I was a stranger, and ye took me not in; naked, and ye clothed me not;

sick, and in prison, and ye visited me not." Oh you willing
and obedient slaves, how long will you be traitors to liberty
and rebels against God? For shame, arise, and shake off your
chains. It is you that stand between the southern slave and his
liberty. It is you that have held him there for 68 years. Dare
you make any pretensions to liberty or honesty while you are
holding these men and women till the planters of the south
can rob and plunder them? Dare you make any pretensions to
the Christian religion while members of that body are sold to
support the church? Who is the God that you worship? Is he
a God of slavery, or a God of liberty? "No man can serve two
masters; for either he will hate the one and love the other, or
else he will hold to the one and despise the other. Ye cannot
serve God and Mammon." "He that says he loves God whom
he has not seen, and hates his brother whom he has seen, is a
liar, and the truth is not in him." Where is the love that you
have shown for the oppressed of your country? Is it for your
adherence to that Constitution, which, I declared before, con-
tains and tolerates the blackest code of laws now in existence?
Your prayers and your petitions are alike; the one mockery to
God, the other an insult.

I do not mean to cast any reflection on the Quakers, for
they have done more than any other sect for the African race;
and there are but few, if any, among them who have any rev-
erence for that devil in sheepskin called the Constitution of
the United States—the great chain that binds the north and
south together, a union to rob and plunder the sons of Africa,

a union cemented with human blood, and blackened with the guilt of 68 years. Ye northern slaves and petty tyrants, how long will you be driven by your southern masters? How long will your homes be the hunting-ground of slaveholders? Do you ever expect to have one foot of ground under the American flag sacred to liberty? Such you have not now; and you dare not claim it. Do you ever expect to see the day when every man can sit under his own vine and fig-tree among you, and no one to molest or make him afraid? Do you ever expect to see the day when the stranger and sojourner with you will not be dragged from your doors? Do you believe that God holds you guiltless of the blood of the three million slaves? The people of the north cannot plead ignorance to the sin of slavery; and, let their opinion have been what it may before the passing of the Fugitive Slave Bill, they can no longer say, "This sin does not lie at my door;" they can no longer say, "I am not my brother's keeper." The blood of your coloured countrymen cries out against you—the laws of God condemn you. The civilised and Christian world is arrayed against slavery. Let them build their ramparts as high as they please, they must and will be pulled down, and the oppressed let go free.

TEN

The Agreement between the North and South at the Adoption of the Constitution

At the time when the Constitution of the United States was adopted, Massachusetts was the only free State in the Union, though several other States were looking for the day when they would be freed from this curse. Georgia, North Carolina, and South Carolina were the three principal States that were in favour of perpetual slavery. The debates in Congress show beyond all doubt that those States would not unite with the other States until Congress passed certain laws to secure to them the right of property in their slaves in any of the States, and other laws of a similar character. It is very evident that those men who framed the Constitution of the United States, felt that they were doing deeds disgraceful and unjust. They hid it as much as possible from the eyes of the world by giving the word "slave" a pleasanter name. It is "person" or "persons" throughout the Constitution.

ELEVEN

The Declaration of American Independence, with Interlineations of United States and State Laws

When, in the course of human events, it becomes necessary for one people to dissolve the political bonds which have connected them with another, and to assume among the powers of the earth the separate and equal station to which the laws of nature and of nature's God entitle them, a decent respect to the opinions of mankind requires that they should declare the causes which impel them to the separation.

"We hold these truths to be self-evident:—That all men are created equal; that they are endowed by their Creator with certain unalienable rights; that among these are life, liberty, and the pursuit of happiness. That no slave held to service or labour in one State, under the laws thereof, escaping into another shall, in consequence of any law or regulation therein, be discharged from such service or labour; but shall be delivered up on claim of the party to whom such service or labour may be due. To secure these rights, governments are instituted among men, deriving their just powers from the consent of the governed, excluding Indians and free negroes. That whenever any form of government becomes destructive of these

ends, it is the right of the people to provide that no amendment which may be made prior to the year one thousand eight
hundred and eight, shall in any manner affect the legalisation
of the slave trade, between the United States and the Coast
of Africa, a part of the price of the Union, paid to the South
by Congress, in 1787. To alter or to abolish it, and to institute
a new provision: any person maliciously killing or dismem-
bering a slave, shall be made to suffer the same punishment as
if the acts had been committed on a free white person, except
cases of *insurrection*, or unless such death should happen by
accident in giving such slave *moderate correction*."

With a Constitution and Union like this, what hope of
freedom is there left for the slave? When shown your oppressive laws, you point us to the Congress of the United States,
as if something could be done there. What has Congress ever
done for freedom? In 1808 it stopped the slave trade between
the United States and Africa. When it had done that, there
was not another Act to be found in the Constitution of the
United States that would allow them to take another step
towards freedom. They have opened new markets for the
extension of slavery and increase of the slave power.

John C. Calhoun, in speaking of the rights of the south,
in a speech he made in Congress, said:—"So long as the
States confine themselves to the exercise of constitutional
rights, they are to be secured from any direct interference,"
which nobody denies; "but, also, that they are entitled to the
direct countenance and support of the general Government

in everything which they are constitutionally entitled to do, even though they may see fit to adopt or to persevere in an obsolete, retrograde, barbarous course of policy, alike disastrous to themselves, and disgraceful to the nation." Mr. Smith, of South Carolina, in the Congress of the United States, said, "To let the slaves loose would be a curse to them. A plan had been thought of in Virginia of shipping them off as soon as they were freed, and this was called humanity. Jefferson's scheme for gradual emancipation, as set forth, in his notes upon Virginia, was derided as impracticable. Emancipation would probably result in an exterminating war. If, on the other hand, a mixture of blood should take place, we should all be mulattoes. The very advocates of manumission held the blacks in contempt, and refused to associate with them. No scheme could be devised to stop the increase of the blacks, except a law to prevent the intercourse of the sexes, or Herod's scheme of putting the children to *death*. The toleration of slavery was said to bring down reproach upon America: but that reproach belongs only to those who tolerate it, and he was ready to bear his share."

Mr. Smith seemed to be greatly alarmed at the idea of amalgamation—while the blood of American statesmen, from the President downwards, has been sold in the slave markets of the south. Look at the many colours between the European and African races, and you have the proof of this assertion at once.

Andrew Jackson, of Tennessee, speaking on the same

question, said—"It is the fashion of the day to favour the liberty of slaves; he believed them better off as they are, and better off than they had been in Africa. Experience had shown that liberated slaves would not work for a living."

These reasons why slavery should not be abolished no longer stand good. Several of the States, soon after the adoption of the Constitution of the United States passed laws for the abolition of slavery in their respective States. The coloured people have not got their rights yet in any of them, as a white citizen. Yet the world must acknowledge, that they can and do take care of themselves, in all the disadvantages they have to labour under. Yet they do not take more than an equal share of gaol or poor-house room from their white brethren. The chances of getting work are, at least, two to one against them. Sailors, mechanics, or day labourers, it is all the same. With all these obstacles in their way, if they can support themselves and families, what might they not do that others have done, if they lived in a free Christian country? I am aware that there are thousands in the States daily offering up their prayers to the God of the oppressed, and using all other means in their power to help the slave whenever he comes within the reach of their mercy; but under the present Constitution of the United States Congress has no power over slavery in the States where it now exists, and to so amend the Constitution as to make it abolish slavery is next to impossible. The following is an article of the amendment, copied from the Constitution:—

"Article 5. The Congress, whenever two-thirds of both Houses deem it necessary, shall propose amendments to this Constitution; or on the application of the Legislatures of two-thirds of the several States, shall call a convention for proposing amendments, which in either case shall be valid to all intents and purposes as part of this Constitution when ratified by the Legislatures of three-fourths of the several States, or by convention, in three-fourths thereof, as the one or the other mode of ratification may be proposed by the Congress, provided that no amendment which may be made prior to the year one thousand eight hundred and eight, shall in any manner affect the first and fourth clauses in the ninth section of the first article, and that no State without its consent shall be deprived of its equal suffrage in the Senate."

The first and fourth clauses in the ninth section of the first article referred to in the Constitution of the United States, shows that the Americans were not ignorant of the enormity of the crime that they were committing. For the first twenty years of their independence, had an angel come from heaven, and pleaded the cause of the slave, they had sworn to hear him not. For that length of time, they had agreed with the kidnappers to protect them in robbing Africa of her sons and daughters. But, after the expiration of these twenty years, which ended in eighteen hundred and eight, that traffic which was the corner-stone of the edifice of American republicanism, was considered a crime worthy of death. I am not learned enough to make that nice distinction between two thieves that

some men can. If a man steals my horse, he is a horse-thief;
but if he steals me from my mother, why he is a respectable
slaveholder, a member of Congress, or President of the United
States; while in fact he is as far beneath the horse-thief as I am
above a horse. I cannot agree with that statesman who said
"what the law makes property, is property." What is law, but
the will of the people—a mirror to reflect a nation's character?
Robbery is robbery, it matters not whether it was done by one
man or a million, whether they were organised or disorgan-
ised: the principle is the same. No law, unless there be one that
can change my nature, can make property of me. Freedom is
as natural for man as the air he breathes, and he who robs
him of his freedom, is also guilty of murder; for he has robbed
him of his natural existence. On this subject the Church and
the State are alike. One will tell a lie, and the other will swear
to it. The State says, "that which the law makes property, is
property." The Church says, "that organic sin is no sin at all;"
both parties having reference to slavery. With a few excep-
tions, their politics and religion are alike oppressive, and rotten and false. None but political tyrants would ever establish
slavery, and none but religious hypocrites would ever support
it. What says Matthew, 15th chapter, 8th and 9th verses:—
"This people draweth nigh unto me with their mouth, and
honoureth me with their lips, but their heart is far from me,
but in vain they worship me, teaching for doctrines the com-
mandments of men."

At the time when the Constitution of the United States

was adopted there were but thirteen States in the Union, with more humanity and less hypocrisy than what there is at the present day, with more than twice the number of States and six times the number of people. It was then slavery struggled for its existence, and had not the friends of liberty compromised principle for power it would before this have been numbered among the things that were; but as an inducement to get the Southern States in the Union they were then forming between the several States, a bill was passed of this nature:— "That no future law that may hereafter be passed by the Congress of the United States shall in any manner affect the slave trade now being carried on between the United States and the Coast of Africa, before the year one thousand eight hundred and eight;" giving the South twenty years to import what slaves they wanted into the country; and the number of slaves has increased to upwards of three millions, over which Congress has no control. The States where slavery exists, are the only ones that can make laws for its regulation; and they being so nearly equal in number with the northern States, and with but one feeling on the subject of slavery, it is impossible for the people of the north to effect any change in the Constitution of the United States that would make it favour freedom. The Union was agreed to for the protection of slavery, without which it could not have existed, and even now, as it has been stated in Congress by slaveholders, a dissolution of the Union would be a dissolution of slavery; but the people of the north dare not contend for their own rights. Six hundred thousand legalised robbers rule the country; the laws of the south are paramount over those of the United States. For proof:—The law of the United States pledges its protection to its citizens going from one State into another. On several occasions men have been taken out of northern ships while lying in southern ports, and sent to gaol for no other crime than having a coloured skin; and whenever the captain of the ship failed to pay the expenses of the prisoner, and take him on board when ready for sea, he was sold into slavery. This baneful kidnapping is carried on up to this day. The people of Massachusetts being unwilling to submit longer to so great and unlawful a wrong, petitioned the Legislature of their State to investigate the matter, and, as soon as possible, to bring it before the Congress of the United States. Two of her most respectable citizens were chosen, and sent to the south with official documents stating the nature of their business, which was to test the legality of a law that had made slaves of men that were born free in other States, and entitled to their protection. What did it all amount to? The south drove them home, and one of them, an elderly gentleman, barely escaped with his life. This is the treatment the south gave the north in the latter part of 1847–8. They received it like slaves.

In eighteen hundred and fifty it came to the slaveholders' turn to ask, or rather to demand. Some of the States had refused them the use of their gaols to put their slaves in. The people would give them food and shelter. They asked Congress to unlock the gaols of the north to them, for the reception of their slaves, and punish every man and woman who would dare give aid to any fugitive. Congress granted them all this; yes, and more. "The people of the north shall catch slaves for you. Wherever our Stars and Stripes fly, there the slave power shall be felt, and freedom shall be driven beyond the bounds of our country, to seek a home among those who have the courage to defend it." The people of the north have not. In the City of Boston, the capital of the State that received the insult from the south, the troops were called out by the Mayor of that city to prevent the escape of a slave. They have taken up arms to force men into slavery, but dare not lift a finger for liberty.

What is to be hoped of a people like this? They are full of lies and hypocrisy. They sell their brother, child, or sister, and if it were possible, I believe they would sell their God, and worship the gold. Give me liberty with a cannibal, rather than slavery with a professed Christian. No man should hold unlimited power over his fellow-man. From the repeated abuses of this power, he becomes the most brutal wretch that ever disgraced the human species; and the more he himself has been abused, the more eager he is to abuse others. But slavery is unnatural, and it requires unnatural means to support it. Everything droops that feels its sting. Hope grows dimmer and dimmer until life becomes bitter and burthensome. At last death frees the slave from his chains, but his wrongs are forgotten. He was oppressed, robbed, and murdered. Better would it be for the slaves, if they must submit to slavery, if the immortal part of them were blotted out;

but, no—the feeling is natural. Nature's God has breathed it into the soul of man, but slavery is the unnatural offspring of hell—a curse to the human family; hated and shunned by all. Rather let us blot that out of existence which stands between man and his rights; God and His laws; the world and its progress. The Christian religion that binds heart to heart, and hand to hand, and makes each and every man a brother, is at war with it; and shall we, whose very souls it has wrung out, be longer at peace? If possible, let us make those whom we have left behind feel that the ground they till is cursed with slavery, the air they breathe poisoned with its venom breath, and that which made life dear to them lost and gone.

In conclusion, let me say that the experience of the past, the present feeling, and, above all this, the promise of God, assure me that the oppressor's rod shall be broken. But how it is to be done has been the question among our friends for years. After the prayers of twenty-five years the slaves' chains are tighter than they were before, their escape more dangerous, and their cups of misery filled nearer its brim. Since I cannot forget that I was a slave, I will not forget those that are slaves. What I would have done for my liberty I am willing to do for theirs, whenever I can see them ready to fill a freeman's grave, rather than wear a tyrant's chain. The day must come; it will come. Human nature will be human nature; crush it as you may, it changes not; but woe to that country where the sun of liberty has to rise up out of a sea of blood. When I have thought of all that would pain the eye, sicken the heart, and make us turn our backs to the scene and weep, I then think of the oppressed struggling with their oppressors, and have a scene more horrible still. But I must drop this subject; I do not like to think of the past, nor look to the future, of wrongs like these. God save us from the blood of the innocent; I ask nothing more.